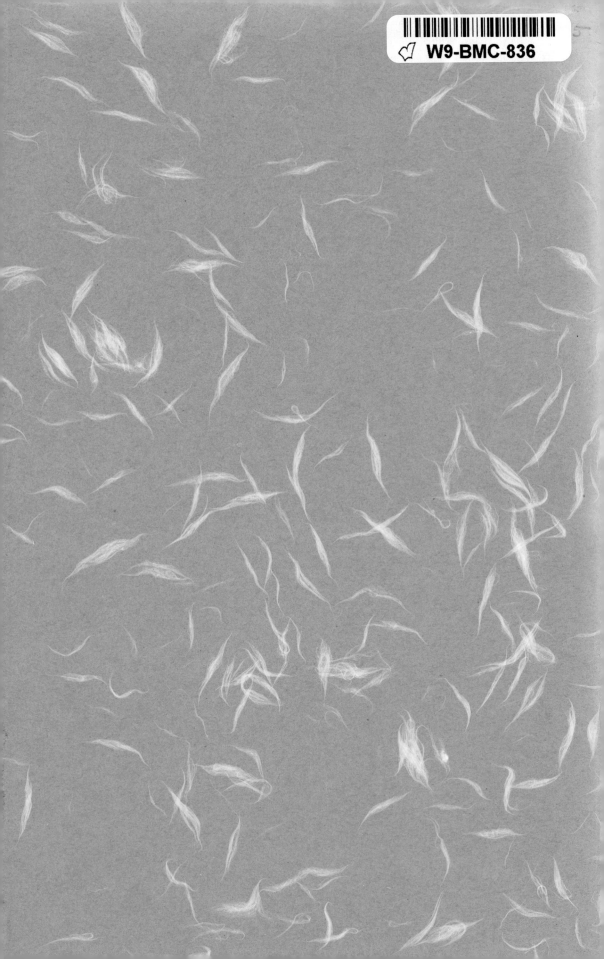

W9-BMC-836

Christmas 1961
From: Polly & Alan
Mrs. Deirdre Thompson
South Legrand Road

Stepping Stones
to
Japanese Floral Art

Rachel E. Carr

Stepping Stones
to
Japanese Floral Art

by

Rachel E. Carr

Published by

TOKYO NEWS SERVICE, LTD.

Kosoku Doro Bldg.
10 Ginza Nishi 8-chome, Chuo-ku,
Tokyo, Japan

No part of this book may be reprinted in any form
without written permission of the publisher or author.

First Edition .. .. August 1955
Second Printing .. .. May 1956
Third Printing .. .. April 1957
Fourth Revised and Enlarged Edition November 1957
Fifth Printing .. .. July 1958
Sixth Edition .. .. July 1959
Seventh Edition .. .. January 1960
Eighth Edition .. .. June 1960

United States Library of Congress Catalog Card Number: 57–10621

Printed in Japan

by

TOKYO NEWS SERVICE, LTD.

Ginza Nishi, Tokyo

To my husband, Bill

"Flowers seem intended for the solace of ordinary humanity; children love them; quiet, tender, cultivated, ordinary people love them as they grow; luxurious and disorderly people rejoice in them gathered."—John Ruskin

ACKNOWLEDGEMENTS

To the Japanese masters of floral art, Mr. Sofu Teshigahara and Mr. Rifuku Enomoto, I wish to express my appreciation for the opportunity to study in their schools, and for having received their personal guidance during the course of my prolonged studies.

I am also indebted to Miss Rikei Yoshida for her invaluable assistance. Also to the late Mr. Shoshun Otake for collaborating on the diagrams and sketches; and to Mr. Heiichi Hashimoto and my husband for their untiring efforts in photographing the arrangements.

To Mrs. Hazel Gorham, I owe my gratitude for her helpful suggestions in the preparation of this book.

日本のいけばふが今日極く外国人にようこばれをることは戦前戦後を通して

みを。ただ賣てふかつたように思はれる。終戦直後アメリカ側の

懇望より　進駐軍将校夫人達に　私が草月流のいけばふを

敷へ始めたのをきつかけに　外人のいけばふ熱が華抗ずくくる

のはまことによろこばしいことである。

然し特に熱心ふ研究をつづける人は極々稀である。

三世人カーはこの稀ふ都に展する人で　バンカース、クラブから引接を

私の敷場にも来られ、特に熱心ふ勉強された。外恵人に稀ふ極番用

ふ英は、多物静かふ性格や落ついた趣味のよう等からもふ東洋

的ふ筆にさえ愛する。既ふ草月流佛範の資格を持つておられる夫人が

こすな「日本のいけばふ」と題して自化のいけばふ写真集を築表され

同好の吉のよう手引とふること、この熱心ふ勉強かよき寅を結は逆

たることたいによろこばしい次れである。

勅使！の河　萬豊風

The extent to which *ikebana,* or the art of Japanese flower arrangement, so greatly enjoyed by foreigners today is, I believe, a phenomenon not previously observed in pre-war Japan.

Shortly after World War II, through the good offices of the American authorities, I was asked to teach the wives of officers of the American forces in Tokyo. The Sogetsu School is widespread, and it is indeed gratifying to note the ever increasing interest among foreigners in *ikebana.*

However, a person who continues to study with keen enthusiasm is rarely found among occidentals. Rachel Carr is one of those persons. Her deftness, coupled with a calm personality and serene good taste, produces something rather oriental about her work. She has received a teacher's diploma from the Sogetsu School.

Mrs. Carr has compiled a group of her own flower arrangements to serve as a guide book. I am more than glad that her earnest study has borne fruit.

SOFU TESHIGAHARA

Founder of the Sogetsu School
of Japanese Flower Arrangement

June 1954
Tokyo, Japan

(Translation of Japanese Text)

いけばなは古来より日本独特の芸術としてその時代々の建築様式を伴って発達してまいりました そして

現今に於きましては一般の人々の日常生活となくてはならないものと迄なってゐると申しても過言で

はないでせう 又第二次大戦後は来日中の各国婦人間も大層愛好されて居ります

この度 カー夫人がその日本のいけばなを大変解り易く皆様々御紹介下さいますことは私共日本の

華道人として華道弘通に於て国際親善の一役を担ふことと誠に欣快に堪えません

カー夫人は一九五二年六月々私共のスクールに入門され以来古流生華及松源流投入盛花を研究され既々

免許を受けて居られますがその豊かな構想と色彩感覚のすぐれてゐる点は誠に日本の生徒達の及ば

ないものがあります 又人一倍の努力家でいけばなの歴史まで勉強され純日本的な古風なスタイルを

花々ついては特に好んで研究されて居られます この度本書に発表されました作品々つきましては日本

いけばなの特徴である天地人の役枝を巧々応用して洋室にもよく調和する様構成されて居り表現法

を於ても大変結構に存じます 何卒本書を御覧になる皆様が早速日本のいけばなを日常生活の中に

取り入れて下さいますれば私共日本の華道人として幸甚それ々過ぎるものはございません

一九五四年九月

古流・松源流　家元　榎本理福

その度再版を当りまして カー夫人がその後たゆまぬ努力の結果、優秀なる成績のもとに
去る四月二十二日美術クラブに於ける当流春季免状授興式々理念の雅韓にて古流生華及び松源流
投入盛花の師範免状を受けられましたことを玆に附記致します

一九五六年四月二十六日
明流神宮前寓居に於て家元理福 記

For centuries the art of Japanese flower arrangement has developed as an important art of Japan along with the advancement of architecture and cultural art in general.

Flower arranging is indispensable in the every-day life of the Japanese. We are proud to acknowledge that after World War II Japanese floral art has been greatly admired by foreigners of all nationalities in Japan.

Rachel Carr's book on Japanese flower arrangements explains this subject with clarity and simplicity. We artists of this field feel very happy that we can do our part toward international goodwill through her book.

Since Mrs. Carr entered the Koryu School she has made a careful study in every technique of Japanese *ikebana*, for which she has received diplomas. Her excellent conception of Oriental art and color harmony is above the reach of many Japanese pupils. She has made a special study of the *Seika* style of flower arrangements. The illustrations in her book are all excellent in their artistic presentation of the principles of Japanese floral designs.

At a graduation ceremony on April 22, 1956, Rachel Carr received Master's Degrees (*Shihan*) for the three styles in Japanese flower arrangement—Seika, Moribana and Nageire. She is the first occidental to be awarded the *Shihan* diploma in Japanese classical flower arrangement from the Koryu School.

RIFUKU ENOMOTO
Grand Master of the
Koryu and Shogen Schools

May 1956
Tokyo, Japan

(Translation of Japanese Text)

Rachel Carr receiving her *Shihan* diplomas from Mr. Rifuku Enomoto, Grand Master of the Koryu and Shogen Schools.

Rachel Carr was born and educated in China. She is married to the former Olympic 400-meter track star, William A. Carr.

The author has spent a number of years in Japan in intensive study of the language and several phases of Japanese art. She is also accomplished in *bonseki*, the art of sand painting, *bonkei*, miniature landscaping, and the creation of Japanese dolls. In addition to her knowledge of Chinese and Japanese, Mrs. Carr speaks several European languages.

Rachel Carr is the author of *A Year of Flowers*, and a forthcoming book, *Japanese Flower Arrangement—Symbolism, Cult and Practice*. She is well-known for her articles and columns in the Asahi Evening News of Tokyo, Hong Kong Standard, Honolulu Advertiser, San Francisco Chronicle, the New York Times, New Zealand Woman's Weekly and the Manila Times. Her work has also appeared in national American magazines—House Beautiful, Woman's Day and Ladies' Home Journal.

THE CRITICS SAID OF AN EARLIER EDITION :

"Any enterprising reader when faced by these inviting pages will probably feel an immediate urge to try his hand."

Nippon Times

"*Stepping Stones to Japanese Floral Art* is presented in recipe form so simple that it would seem anyone who can read, can create a flower arrangement of great beauty."

The Mainichi

"Of all the books on flower arranging, Rachel Carr's *Stepping Stones to Japanese Floral Art* is the most readable and the most interesting."

Pacific Stars & Stripes

"Rachel Carr has done a very commendable job with her method of treatment of this subject. It is refreshing to find a 'do it yourself' book in English on a traditionally Japanese art. Anyone with some inherent artistic ability, manual skill and imagination should derive a great deal of pleasure from this concisely presented introduction to the art of saying more with flowers."

Asahi Evening News

"When this book was shown to a woman in her eighties, she looked it over carefully and exclaimed, "If I were ten years younger, I would go through this book lesson by lesson! Even now, I can hardly resist; it is so carefully and interestingly worked out."

Contemporary Japan

"*Stepping Stones to Japanese Floral Art* is an exceptionally well-illustrated and informative volume, enabling the foreigner to appreciate and become adept in floral arrangement. It is, as the title suggests, a step by step initiation of this fascinating Japanese study."

South China Morning Post, Hong Kong

"*Stepping Stones to Japanese Floral Art* cannot be praised too highly. It is a truly delightful book. Its beauty commends it as a gift and its practicality assures it a place on every bookshelf."

Hong Kong Tiger Standard

"Graceful, fluid motion keynotes most of Rachel Carr's arrangements in *Stepping Stones to Japanese Floral Art*. Each piece of material is carefully placed to form a definite relationship to the whole, and the overall impression is of strength and dignity without stiffness, of balance without strain, and of beauty without contrivance."

Art in Flowers, New York

"Along with the Oriental influence on American interior design, it is fitting to bring to light a splendid book on Japanese flower arrangements, *Stepping Stones to Japanese Floral Art* by Rachel E. Carr. Mrs. Carr gives the fascinating history of Japanese floral art in simple detail. Then she goes on to describe the basic equipment, measurements and techniques with a great feeling of Oriental delicacy. Illustrated arrangements in three different styles are accompanied by pen-and-ink sketches. By studying these readers can duplicate somewhat the author's talents. The arrangements alone are beautiful, but the sketches make the book valuable for practical study."

New York Times

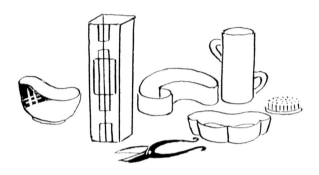

This book is designed as a simple and direct approach to the art of Japanese flower arrangement. Each floral study is basic in structure, and the substitutes given for containers and plant materials will permit variations in the arrangements and stimulate your own creative resources. To supplement the partial loss of depth and perspective in a photograph, expanded drawings with a circle of numbers are given to indicate the relative positions of each line in the designs.

The restrained beauty, depth, simplicity and arrested rhythm so typical of Japanese flower arrangements, are contrived by the use of a modicum of flowers and branches harmoniously related to each other and to the container.

The different seasons are expressed, and the characteristic habitat of each plant is depicted in an arrangement. The water surface is regarded as the soil from which the flowers and branches emerge. Rustic and woody scenes are captured by a symbolic tree towering above a low grouping of flowers and greenery that represent the fields and valleys. In a waterside study can be found reeds, irises and water lilies grouped ingeniously to give the illusion of natural growth in miniature scale. There are also floral studies in which the natural association of plant materials is not maintained, rather form and texture are dramatized.

There is rich symbolism in Japanese flower arrangements. The most symbolic aspect is the philosophy of *In* and *Yō*, the negative and positive elements which govern the universe in Oriental cosmology. *Yō* is the positive element, and is the giver of life. *In*, the negative element, is the receiver of life. *Yō* expresses the masculine features of strength and roughness, the brightness of the sun, and plants that have reached a stage of maturity. *In* expresses the feminine features of weakness and softness, the coolness of the moon, and plants in budded stages. The obverse of a leaf, which is the bright side, is *Yō*. The dark, reverse side of a leaf is *In*. The right and left sides of a divided midrib in a leaf are also significant of *In* and *Yō*. The observance of these two cosmic forces is more evident in the classical Seika style of arranging flowers than in the modern Moribana and Nageire styles. The interplay in the balance of opposites, light and shade, stages of development and textural contrasts precludes monotony and symmetry. The evidence of these tenets can be found in all phases of Japanese art.

As in sculpture or painting, knowledge of the principles of design and technique is the very backbone of a good composition. The application of these principles when strengthened by patience and study will reflect the artist's own creativeness. Working in a quiet atmosphere, with a planned idea in mind, will bring success in the arrangements you aspire to do.

Rachel E. Carr

CONTENTS

ILLUSTRATIONS

MORIBANA—**Naturalistic Style**

HISTORICAL SKETCH

Ikebana, or the art of arranging flowers in Japan, has been built on centuries of study, reflection and creation. It is one of the four ancient cultural accomplishments of tea ceremony, incense burning, and sand painting.

The roots of Japanese flower arrangement trace back to India where offering of flowers to the gods in altar worship became an integral part of Buddhistic ceremonies. When Buddhism infiltrated China in the first centuries A.D., floral altar decorations were introduced at the same time. The early influences of these designs can be found in their paintings, porcelains, ivory, and other arts. Floral designs soon became a dominant force in Chinese culture.

In the sixth century the Prince Regent of Japan, Shotoku-Taishi, sent envoys to China for cultural guidance. One of the envoys was an Imperial member of the court, Ono-no-imoko, who brought back with him the concepts of Chinese secular culture along with an appreciation of the Buddhistic practice of floral altar worship.

After the death of the Prince Regent, Ono-no-imoko terminated his imperial duties with the court and retired to a small hut by the side of a lake to pray for the departed soul of the Prince. When he was appointed guardian of the temple Rokkaku-do in Kyoto, much of his time was devoted to arranging flowers for altar worship. He formulated basic rules with stylized designs, thus bringing into existence the first known flower arrangement school—*Ikenobo*. The characters *ike-no-bo* mean "hermit by the lake", a name bestowed on him by his disciples.

The principal building of the *Ikenobo* School still stands on the same site of the ancient historic temple. This school has great prestige in the eyes of the Japanese.

As the religion of Buddhism spread in Japan, the priests of the temples devoted much time to the study of floral designs. They evolved a system of arranging flowers more artistically and developed formal and elaborate designs, heavily vested in rituals and religious concepts.

The designs were based on a structural triad. The tallest line symbolized *Heaven*. The secondary line was identified as *Man*, and the tertiary line, as *Earth*. This triad reflected the teachings of Confucius:

Heaven, as the soul of all elements of life, *Man*, the fundamental way by which all things become active, and *Earth*, the way in which all things take form."

A seventeenth century print showing a Buddhist monk
executing a *Rikkwa* arrangement

The celebrated Captain Brinkley in his book, *A History of the Japanese People*, expressed very well the evolution in Japan of the art of arranging flowers: "What the Buddhists imported from India was based on equality of distribution—what the Japanese conceived was a method based on balance of inequalities".

In the ninth century the art of arranging flowers spread from the temples to the courts of the nobles and feudal lords.

Over a period of centuries innumerable schools and styles evolved from the ancient *Ikenobo* School. Some of the styles taught were extremely simple, expressing the natural growth of plant life, while others showed a tendency toward exaggerated curves, giving an unnatural appearance to the floral designs.

Zen, a sect of Buddhism, had a great influence on floral designs. It was the Zen doctrines of simplicity in living and love of nature that influenced the art of arranging flowers into a more expressive form, suggestive of flowers in their natural state. Zen doctrines which demanded daily meditation by its followers, led to the creation of the *tokonoma* (place of honor) in a Japanese home. Also a place of aesthetic beauty, the *tokonoma* is graced by a fine painting or calligraphy, an incense burner, and a flower arrangement.

In the fifteenth century floral art, tea cult, incense burning, sand painting, and other ancient arts were advanced in great strides by Shogun Yoshimasa, a munificent patron of all arts. Tired of mundane affairs, Yoshimasa retired to the renowned Silver Pavilion in Kyoto, and there he dedicated the rest of his life to the perfection of Japanese arts.

The practice of arranging flowers as an expressive art became the common heritage of all classes of Japanese during the Meiji Restoration. It is interesting to note that the most famous masters have all been men.

Old woodblock print showing a tea ceremony in front of a *tokonoma*

The recorded history of Japanese floral art indicates that certain styles have exerted strong influences on the development of the art to its present form. Of these the most significant are: *Rikkwa*, *Heika* (also known as *Nageire*), *Chabana*, *Seika* and *Moribana*.

RIKKWA —

"Standing up Plant Cuttings"

The *Rikkwa* style was the first distinctive form of arrangement developed from the early altar styles by the *Ikenobo* masters. The arrangement suggested nature in its entirety, producing a landscape effect. A variety of floral materials were required to recreate mountains, waterfalls, streams and other facets of nature. Chinese landscape paintings were used as an inspiration to reproduce similar ideas. The style was large, formal, and elaborate, and stood over six feet in height. The arrangements sometimes took several days to create, and required a great deal of skill. The containers used were heavy bronze vases. Wisps of straw supported the plant materials. This style is now seldom seen at Japanese floral exhibitions.

HEIKA —

"Vase Flowers"

In the twelfth century a style known as *Heika* developed. Flowers and branches were arranged with simplicity and the compositions were smaller in height than the *Rikkwa* form.

Nageire, which developed after *Heika*, expressed the natural growth of plants. These two styles have now merged into one, and are known by either name. It was in this period that flowers began to be used in the homes for decorations.

CHABANA —

"Flowers for Tea Ceremony"

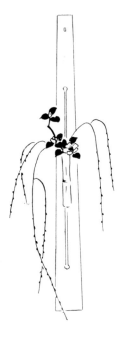

In the latter part of the sixteenth century the masters of tea ceremony, another ancient Japanese culture, made their contribution to the evolution of floral art. As part of the tea ceremony, which exemplifies the communion of man with nature, they adopted extremely simple arrangements often consisting of one or two flowers in a plain container. One's emotions are often stirred by the exquisite beauty of so delicate a flower arrangement. This style was named *Chabana*.

"Alive Flowers"

The elegant *Seika* is the formal or traditional style of Japanese flower arrangement. This style is based on a distinct tri-lineal pattern. Each school has its own fundamental rules which vary slightly, but the overall effect is strikingly similar. *Seika* is extremely demanding in that the apparent simplicity of the well-defined Heaven-Man-Earth lines is the result of precise relative measurements and carefully balanced curves. Although these lines have a strict adherence to a set formal pattern, a sense of tranquility, restraint, and simplicity is expressed. Even though modern containers and needle point holders are used now with this style, the classical form has been maintained.

The *Seika* of the Koryu School has been selected for this book. This school originated in the eighteenth century and its branches are widespread in Japan.

MORIBANA —

"Piled up Flowers"

Toward the end of the nineteenth century a new trend in Japanese flower arrangement developed at the time Japan opened her doors to Western civilization. *Moribana*, the modern style, had a tendency toward a more naturalistic appearance depicting landscapes, miniature ponds and other phases of plant growth. The basic tri-lineal form was still retained but with a greater freedom of expression. Shallow containers of all types are used for this style.

NAGEIRE —

"Thrown in Flowers"

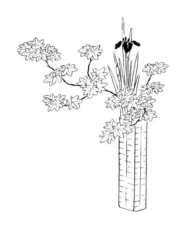

The nineteenth century also influenced the ancient vase-type arrangements known as *Nageire* or *Heika*. While the early vase arrangements were stiff and formal, the modern *Nageire* captures depth and feeling of movement. Modern decorated and glazed vases with bright colors, as well as the conservative types are used today in harmony with the modern artistic tendencies in Japan.

In recent years abstract floral art took its place in the gallery of Japan's wealth of styles.

Innumerable schools in Japan teach both the traditional and modern styles. The *Moribana* and *Nageire* styles illustrated in this book are based on the fundamental principles of the modern Shogen and Sogetsu Schools.

BASIC MEASUREMENTS

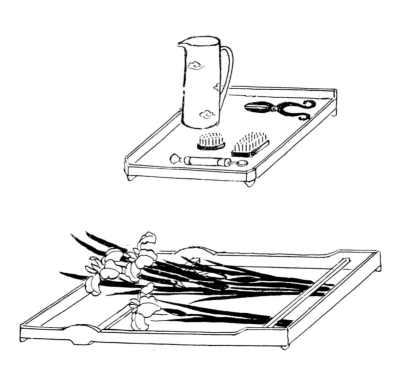

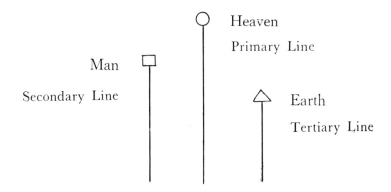

Heaven

Primary Line

Man

Secondary Line

Earth

Tertiary Line

Individual markings are given for the three radical lines of Heaven, Man and Earth to indicate their postions in the basic measurements explained on pages 36, 37 and 38, for the three styles—*Seika, Nageire* and *Moribana*.

In all *Seika* arrangements precise rules and relative heights must be followed. In the modern styles of *Nageire* and *Moribana* these three lines may be arranged freely maintaining, however, the basic asymmetric form.

How to Measure Stems or Branches

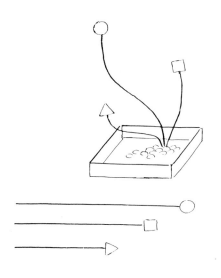

Measure the stems or branches in a straight position. The measurements will appear different after the arrangement is created due to the curving of the lines, but the proportions will be maintained.

When a sense of balance and proportion is acquired through the practice of the basic rules given, precise measurements will then no longer be of major importance. The *Moribana* and *Nageire* styles demand freedom of expression and imagination. However, this is not true of *Seika* arrangements.

How to Use Supplementary Stems or Branches

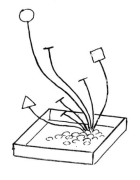

When additional stems or branches are used they become the supplementary lines of the Heaven-Man-Earth basic form. They are always cut shorter than the predominating lines with which they are arranged. The number of supplementary stems or branches used depends on the type of arrangement. For simple arrangements one, two, or three supplementary lines are sufficient; whereas, in larger compositions a greater number would be required. It is important to remember that when using supplementary lines the container should not be crowded. All lines must emerge from a focal point. Simplicity of line is achieved by avoiding mass grouping of floral materials. The general effect is pleasing, graceful and delicate.

Seldom does a Japanese arrangement contain more than two, or possibly three colors in addition to the green of the foliage. This tends to confine the center of interest and emphasize the beauty of the individual flowers.

BASIC MEASUREMENTS FOR *SEIKA*
Traditional Style

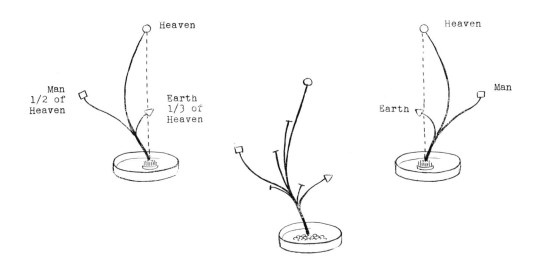

Seika arrangements consist of five basic designs. The simplest and most important one is given in this book. The characteristic of all *Seika* arrangements is that emphasis is placed on the three-line movement. All branches and stems project as a single unit from the surface of the water to form the parent stalk. The appearance of a *Seika* arrangement is destroyed if the lines are spread at the base.

The *Heaven*, or primary line, is the central and tallest line. The tip is drectly above its base, and it assumes the shape of an archer's bow. Exception is made to plants which grow rigidly erect, and are generally arranged in the manner of their growth. The *Man*, or secondary line, and *Earth*, or tertiary line, when curved are approximately one-half and one-third respectively of the *Heaven* line. They are placed to the left and right of the *Heaven* line, and may be interchanged. A guide for the measurement of the *Heaven* line is given in each *Seika* design illustrated in this book.

BASIC MEASUREMENTS FOR *NAGEIRE*

Vase Style

For the *Nageire* style there are three basic measurements which vary with small, medium and large vases.

Small Containers

Heaven : Height of vase plus widest width

Man : 3/4 of Heaven

Earth : 3/4 of Man

Large Containers

Heaven : Twice the height of vase plus widest width

Man : 3/4 of Heaven

Earth : 1/2 of Man

Medium Containers

Heaven : 1 1/2 times height of vase plus widest width

Man : 3/4 of Heaven

Earth : 1/2 of Man

BASIC MEASUREMENTS FOR *MORIBANA*

Naturalistic Style

In the **Moribana** style basic comparative measurements vary with the size of container used.

Small Containers

Heaven: Diameter or length of container plus depth

Man : 3/4 of Heaven

Earth : 3/4 of Man

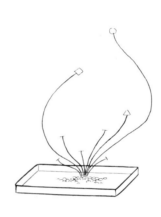

Large Containers

Heaven: Twice the diameter or length of container plus depth

Man : 3/4 of Heaven

Earth : 1/2 of Man

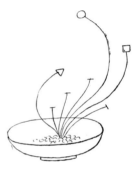

Medium Containers

Heaven: 1 1/2 times diameter or length of container plus depth

Man : 3/4 of Heaven

Earth : 3/4 of Man

PRESERVATION OF CUT PLANTS
AND
FLOWER ARRANGING TECHNIQUES

PRESERVATION OF CUT PLANTS

By following a few simple practices the life of cut plants can be increased and your arrangements kept fresh longer.

After plants have been cut, they should be placed in deep, cool water, away from heat and draft. Garden plants should be cut early morning or late afternoon when evaporation in plant cells is low.

Before starting an arrangement cut the stems diagonally under water. This prevents air from entering the stem, and permits an easier intake of water. At least an inch of the stem should be submerged in water.

Cut plants will last longer if superfluous leaves, flowers, and buds are removed. Leaves submerged in water tend to clog the stems.

Water in an arrangement should be changed daily. For arrangements that can be moved easily, run fresh water into the container until it overflows. A syringe or siphon can be used to drain large containers.

Woody Plants such as chrysanthemum, hydrangea, orchid, rose, wisteria and rhododendron can be treated by either hot water or charring.

Bleeding Plants such as dahlia, hollyhock, poinsettia and poppy can also be treated by either method: hot water or charring. Plants which exude a milky texture should have their ends immersed immediately in hot water or seared; otherwise their latex cells will collapse.

Succulent Plants such as calla lily, tulip, water lily and most spring bulbs should be placed erect in deep water for at least twenty minutes to allow free absorption. Pump cool water into the stems before arranging.

Note There are many conflicting suggestions for handling woody, bleeding and succulent plants. The above treatments are the results of research made with the assistance of Japanese florists, and are the simplest methods of preserving cut plants.

Hot Water Treatment

Cover the foliage and flowers well before immersing in hot water. Leave for about two minutes and then place in a bucket of deep cool water before arranging.

Charring Treatment

When charring, the foliage and flowers should be protected from heat of the flame. Expose not more than two inches of the stem. Then place in a bucket of deep cool water before arranging.

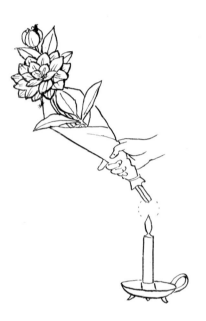

Pump Treatment

Water growing plants are delicate and wither rapidly when removed from their natural habitat. After the stems have been pumped and the flowers arranged, frequent spraying with cool water will increase the life span of the flowers and their foliage.

FLOWER ARRANGING TECHNIQUES

Certain plant materials require the knowledge of specific techniques to enhance their beauty and to secure their balance in an arrangement.

Branches often require bending to give them more expressive lines. Some branches are supple enough and will readily assume the required curve while others of a refractory nature will snap if handled incorrectly. Refractory branches should be saturated, at the places to be bent, with a mild solution of vinegar and hot water. Dip the branch immediately in cold water to set the curve. Branches which are leafy and flowering should be placed directly over a flame, with their foliage and blossoms covered. Hold above candle flame for two or three seconds, repeating several times until the branch becomes supple enough to take the manipulated curve. Then dip immediately in cold water to set the curve.

Fig. 1

How to bend a slender branch

Fig. 2

How to bend a thick branch

Fig. 1 : When curving a slender branch place your thumbs close together and bend gently, repeating the same motion until the desired effect is achieved.

Fig. 2 : When curving a thick branch, grasp it with both hands exerting pressure with your left thumb, and bend with gradual force just short of breaking. Slight incisions on the outer side of a branch where a curve is desired, will induce it to bend without snapping.

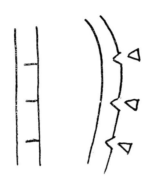

How to bend a branch with a wide diameter

Fig. 3: Branches with a wide diameter can be arched if transverse cuts are made, and triangular pegs of the plant materials inserted to hold the shape of the branch. The pegs should be sawed rather than cut.

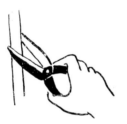

How to cut branch or stem

Fig. 4: When branches and stems are cut diagonally they have certain advantages:

    a. better intake of water

    b. more secure placement in needle point holder

    c. firmer support against wall of vase

How to bend a stem

Fig. 5 : When curving a stem bend gradually. A slight bending and twisting motion, if carefully done, will prevent the stem from snapping. The stem must be bent between the leaves and not at leaf joint.

How to Trim and Groom a Flower

A flower can appear more graceful if it has been trimmed and stripped of its dense leaves. Thought and care should be given to the natural distribution of leaves when trimming.

Three type of flowers are illustrated before and after they have been groomed.

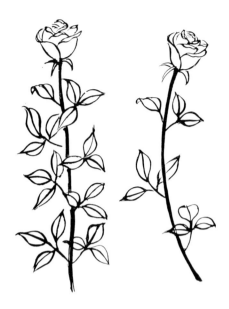

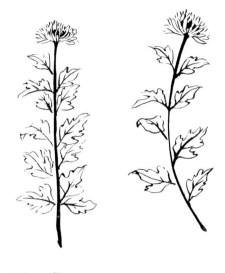

Fig. 7 :

Fig. 6 :

Thorns of the rose have been carefully removed, the leaves trimmed, and the stem curved.

Dense leaves of the chrysanthemums require much trimming to give a delicate appearance to the flower.

Fig. 8 :

Often the gladiolus can take on a new appearance if its long budded spikes are removed, and the leaves regrouped.

How to Trim and Groom a Leafy Branch

Training the eye to trim a leafy branch and bring out its rhythmic lines is one of the most difficult aspects of flower arranging. The novice finds this problem baffling—how much to cut and where. It is important to remember that an uncluttered distribution of leaves and graceful curves play a major part in the make-up of a *finished* arrangement.

Illustrated is a rhododendron branch before and after it has been trimmed and separated. The thick overlapping foliage has little evidence of rhythmic lines. Two sketches are given as examples of the various possible effects that can be derived from the untrimmed branch. Note the sparsity of leaves and the airy appearance they give. The tips taper off with no overlapping leaves.

Fig. 9 :   Untrimmed branch

Fig. 10 :   Branch is trimmed and severed, showing two different effects.

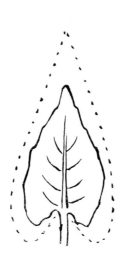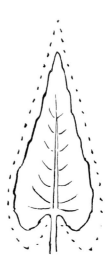

How to reshape a leaf

Fig. 11 :

> Leaves can be reshaped to the size desired by cutting along the margin, and following the natural pattern of the leaf. This is a useful technique when grading leaves in an arrangement.

Fig. 12

Fig. 13

Fig. 14

How to furl a leaf

Fig. 12 : For a tight furl, place the tip of a leaf between your thumb and index finger and roll tightly.

Fig. 13 : For a loose furl, roll the tip of a leaf around a pencil.

Fig. 14 : For more emphatic furls, place the rolled leaf between the palms of your hands and roll in a forward and backward motion till the desired effect has been achieved.

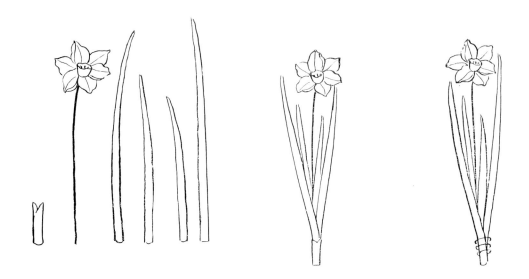

How to groom narcissus and daffodil blades

Fig. 15 : The strap leaves of the narcissus and daffodil can be more artistically arranged if they are separated from their sheaths and regrouped. Place the clump on a flat surface and gently roll the sheath with the palm of your hand. This will enable you to withdraw the leaves without damaging the sheath. Remove inner blades first. When reassembling, place the shorter blades close to the flower stem: this is a characteristic of their growth. Before inserting into the sheath, taper the base so that it will fit into the sheath. If the sheath is damaged, fine florist wire tied at the base will hold the blades and stem together. The wire should be concealed by either pebbles or foliage, depending on the type of arrangement.

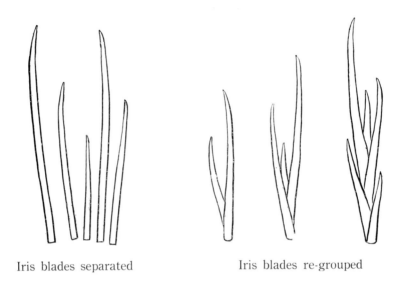

Iris blades separated   Iris blades re-grouped

How to groom iris blades

Fig. 16 : Iris blades can be rearranged to emphasize the beauty of their sword shaped leaves by separating them and reassembling in the shape and height desired. The leaves become an expressive part of an iris composition. In reassembling, the tips of the blades point toward each other in accordance with the natural growth of the plant. Regroup by sliding the blades one into the other, or dampen the base of the group with water and with your thumb and index finger press gently until they adhere. Either method will hold the leaves in a compact unit.

How to Arrange Plant Materials
in a Shallow Container

The needle point holder is the only type used in this book for the *Seika* and *Moribana* styles. Contrary to belief, needle point holders actually increase the life of the plant materials because they open the plant cells and permit an easier absorption of water.

Various techniques are illustrated to give secure support to the holder and plant materials used.

Fig. 17: If the material is too heavy for the holder, place another needle point holder in reverse position at a slant. This will balance even a heavy branch. Modeling clay pressed around the holder is also effective.

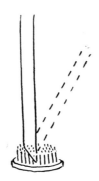

Fig. 18:   Split or crush the end of a thick branch before anchoring it in the needle point holder. Then insert in an upright position and gradually incline to the desired angle. Splitting or crushing the base of a thick branch will not only give the branch a firm support, but will also permit a free intake of water.

Fig. 19: Insert a woody stem within a hollow stem for better support. Firm wire inserted in long, hollow or fleshy stems will prevent drooping.

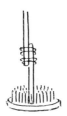

Fig. 20: When a flower has been cut too short, tie it to a longer stem and secure with florist wire. Be sure that the main stem is submerged in at least an inch of water.
This technique can also be applied to slender stems that require firmer support in the holder.

How to Arrange Plant Materials
in a Vase

Vase arrangements of the *Nageire* style are more difficult to accomplish than the shallow container type. Certain techniques are used to anchor tall branches if they present a problem of balance.

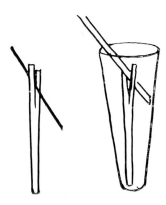

Fig. 21: To secure the balance of any tall branch, this standard technique will be most helpful. For the support, split the tip of a sturdy branch about half an inch in diameter, and cut its base straight so that it will rest securely at the bottom of the vase. The height should be about two inches below the rim of the container.

When placing the main branch in the support, cut its base diagonally to enable it to rest against the wall of the vase. Other floral materials to be used in the arrangement will have their support from the main branch.

Fig. 22: When branches require no support, cut the base at a slant for better balance.

Fig. 23: Another method used for heavy branches. Select a sturdy branch to be used as a support, and measure its length by the width of the vase. Place the support in the container, as illustrated, and force it securely against the inside walls.

BASIC REQUIREMENTS

AND

POINTS TO REMEMBER

BASIC REQUIREMENTS

Needle point holders of various sizes.

Good sharp shears that will not mangle stems.

Spray for watering flowers.

Pump for injecting water in fleshy and hollow stems.

Simple shaped containers of neutral colors.

Pebbles and rocks.

Florist wire.

Keep on hand dry wedges or woody stems for vase supports.

Large plastic tablecloth to save the surface of your work table.

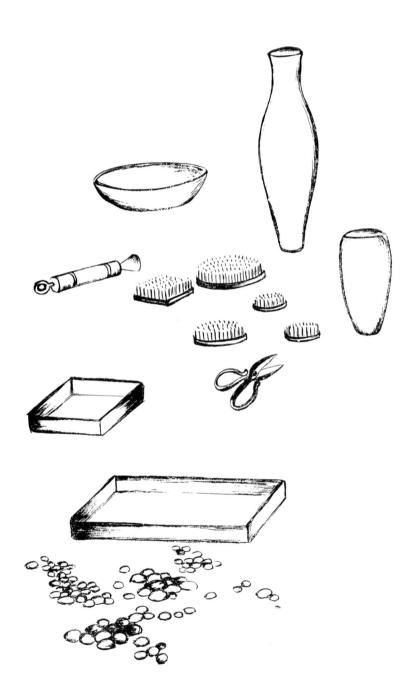

POINTS TO REMEMBER

Japanese arrangements are based on a tri-lineal, asymmetric form.

All lines emerge from a focal point. Lines in the arrangement move forward, backward or to the side but never to the four cardinal points of the compass. They are not placed on the same plane, nor are they of the same height. This creates rhythm and depth, and the visual weight of the irregular lines balances each other.

Line is more important than color in a Japanese design. The emphasis is on form. For beauty of line remove all crossing branches, wilted or excess flowers and foliage. Branches and leaves must be thoroughly cleansed before arranging. Plant material below the surface of the water will tend to rot and thus clog the cells.

Flowers in various stages of development are more interesting than fully matured ones. The Japanese prefer to arrange buds, thereby giving the observer the pleasure of their development.

The container must be well related to the plant materials to create perfect blending of form, color and texture.

Avoid crowding the container.

Accessories should not draw the observer's attention away from the floral design. Rather, they should be in subtle harmony with the arrangement.

The mechanics in a design should be well concealed by foliage, pebbles or rocks.

Spraying an arrangement will not only give it a dewy appearance, but will keep the plant materials fresh longer. Spraying also revives wilted flowers. Keep arrangement away from excessive heat and draft.

Consideration should be given the setting for the arrangement. Correct wall space and height of table surface are of utmost importance. A beautiful arrangement can be destroyed if its beauty is hidden in a cluttered environment.

'Twixt you and me
I placed a rose,
That the flower might share
In love's overflows.

Hiroshi

SEIKA

Traditional Style

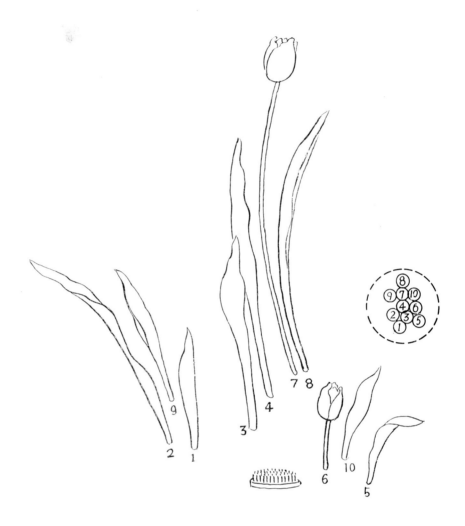

TULIPS

Materials Required

    1.   Round or square container 8″—10″.

    2.   Two tulips and eight leaves.

    3.   Pebbles.

    4.   Medium needle point holder.

Simplicity of line is well expressed in this tranquil study of two tulips rising from a bed of their own foliage. The Chinese cloisonne bowl blends in harmony with the arrangement.

Method of Arrangement

Select tulips in opening bud stages rather than fully matured blossoms. This will not only enhance the arrangement, but will give the flowers a longer life span. Brush petals with the white of an egg to prevent them from opening too wide.

Bend the taller tulip as shown. Trim edges of the leaves if they are torn or too large. Steps 1, 3, 5, 9 and 10 are cut shorter and smaller than Steps 2, 4 and 8. The backs of leaves in Steps 1, 3 and 4 face forward. The foliage should envelop the tulips in the manner of their natural growth. The stems are arranged close together. Conceal the holder with pebbles.

Measurements for the three radical lines :

Heaven line—Step 7. 2 1/2 times the diameter of container.
Man line   —Step 2. 1/2 of Heaven.
Earth line —Step 5. 1/3 of Heaven.

CALLA LILIES

Materials Required

1. Round or square container 10″—12″.
2. Two calla lilies and five leaves.
3. Pebbles.
4. Medium needle point holder.

Dignified calla lilies with their rich foliage emerge elegantly in classic
rhythm from a black lacquer bowl.

Method of Arrangement

For this design, select a bud for the taller lily and a more mature
one for the shorter lily. Curve Step 5 as shown. Firm wire, if inserted
in the stem of the lily, will prevent it from drooping. Trim the leaves of
Steps 1 and 3 to make them smaller than those of Steps 2, 4 and 7.
The backs of leaves in Steps 1 and 4 face forward. The foliage should
overlap to create an effect of a single plant growing from the surface of
the water. Pump the leaves and stems with cool water before arranging.
When the veins of the foliage swell, sufficient water has been pumped
into them. Conceal the holder with pebbles.

Measurements for the three radical lines :

Heaven line—Step 5. Twice the diameter of container.
Man line   —Step 2. 1/2 of Heaven.
Earth line   —Step 3. 1/3 of Heaven.

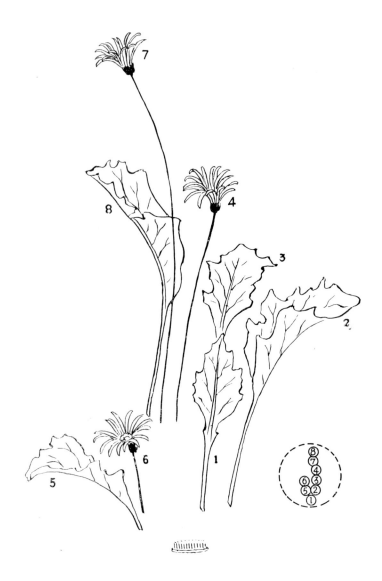

GERBERAS

Materials Required

1. Round or square container 8″—10″.
2. Three gerberas and five leaves.
3. Pebbles.
4. Medium needle point holder.

A study of classic design is expressed by slender spiked gerberas which project from a cluster of their own notched foliage, in a blue porcelain Chinese bowl.

Method of Arrangement

Gerberas are delicate flowers and their stems should be handled carefully when curving. Since the leaves become an expressive part of the arrangement, they should be selected with care. Bruised, torn or large leaves can be trimmed by cutting along the notched edges, following the natural pattern of the leaf.

Curve the stem in Step 7 as shown. Steps 4 and 6 are arranged erect. Leaves in Steps 1, 3 and 5 are trimmed to appear smaller than those in Steps 2 and 8. The backs of leaves in Steps 1 and 3 face forward. If the stems are placed very close together they will give the impression of a single plant rising from the surface of the water. Conceal the holder with pebbles.

Measurements for the three radical lines :

Heaven line—Step 7. 2 1/2 times the diameter of container.
Man line   —Step 2. 1/2 of Heaven.
Earth line —Step 5. 1/3 of Heaven.

(71)

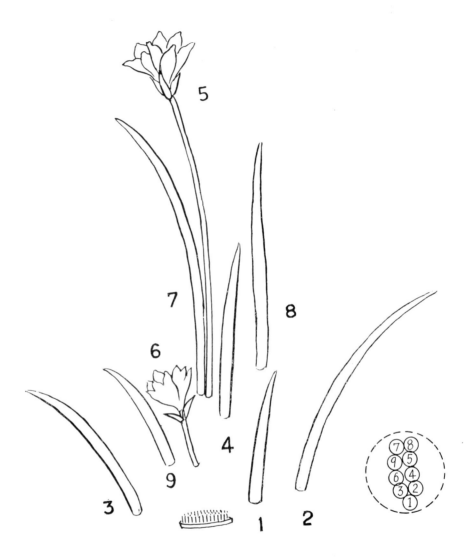

AMARYLLIS

Materials Required

1. Round or square container 10″—12″.
2. Two amaryllis with buds and seven leaves.
3. Pebbles.
4. Medium needle point holder.

Angular lines of striking amaryllis rise briskly erect from their leathery foliage. The porcelain container and lacquer base echo the deep color tones of the arrangement.

Method of Arrangement

Since it is the nature of the amaryllis to grow erect, this characteristic is dramatized in a floral study by giving the leaves expressive lines to soften the rigid stems. Leaves are furled by drawing them between the thumb and index finger in the direction of the curve desired. To produce a more natural effect, the backs of leaves in Steps 1 and 4 face forward. The leaves envelop the blossoms. A more interesting composition is created if blossoms are selected in different stages of development. Conceal the holder with pebbles.

Measurements for the three radical lines :

        Heaven line—Step 5. Twice the diameter of container.
        Man line   —Step 2. 1/2 of Heaven.
        Earth line   —Step 3. 1/3 of Heaven.

CHRYSANTHEMUMS

Materials Required

1. Round or square container 12″—14″.
2. Seven chrysanthemums.
3. Pebbles.
4. Medium needle point holder.

Restrained classic lines are well interpreted through the leafy stems of yellow chrysanthemums, arranged in a black and flaming red lacquer bowl.

Method of Arrangement

Chrysanthemums are difficult to bend. It is best to select naturally curved, long single stems. However, additional bending is necessary to duplicate the lines in the diagrams. Flowers should be in different stages of development. When pruning the dense leaves, the natural effect of leaf distribution should not be destroyed. Note that leaves are removed entirely from the base of the stems. This is necessary in grouping the stems close together to give the impression of a single plant diverging into a tri-lineal form. If wire is used to hold the stems together at the base, it should be completely concealed by lower foliage. Conceal the holder with pebbles.

Measurements for the three radical lines:

Heaven line—Step 6. Twice the diameter of container.
Man line　—Step 1. 1/2 of Heaven.
Earth line　—Step 5. 1/3 of Heaven.

They seem to nod to one another
And whisper face to face,
Morn and eve—the flowers blooming
In th' water of this little vase.

                                    Gyofu

NAGEIRE

Vase Style

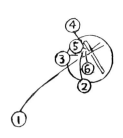

CAMELLIAS

Materials Required

1. Vase 12″—16″ in height.
   Bamboo, lacquer or wooden base.
2. Four camellia branches.
   Substitute : magnolias, rhododendron or loquat.
3. Sprigs of pine, if desired.
4. Short woody stem for support.

Pink camellias lend their beauty to the graceful lines of their branches. The lacquer container and base add their appeal to this sophisticated design.

Method of Arrangement

Cut and trim four separate camellia branches as shown. The foliage should be sparse to set it apart from the blossoms. Steps 1, 2 and 4 form the triangular design. Split the base of Step 1 and insert a woody stem measuring the width of the vase just below the rim. Step 1 faces forward, toward the left. Step 2 is off-center a little to the left, and Step 4 at a backward slant. Sprigs of pine or additional camellia foliage will give added depth to the arrangement.

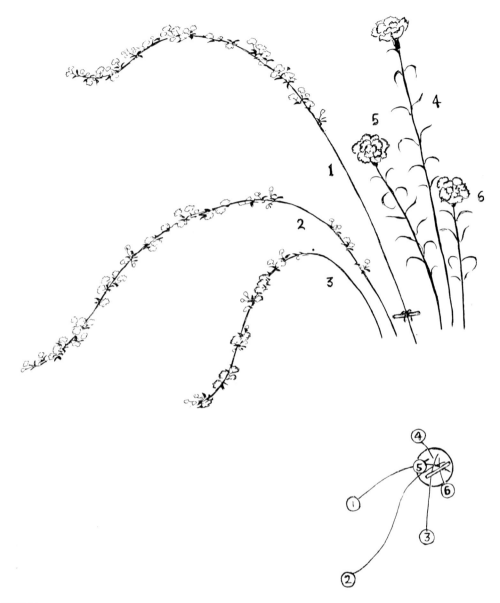

BRIDAL WREATH—CARNATIONS

Materials Required

1. Wall or table type vase 10"—14" in height.
2. Three branches of bridal wreath.
   Substitutes: similar flowering type, willow, ferns, hanging vine or ivy.
3. Three carnations.
   Substitutes: roses, gerberas or daisies.
4. Short woody stem for support.
5. Florist wire.

Slender carnations combined with sprays of
bridal wreath in a bamboo container make a
decorative wall arrangement, enhanced by a
Japanese figurine and ivory fan.

Method of Arrangement

Branches of bridal wreath should be well trimmed to reveal their
delicate lines. First study the branch to find its most expressive lines, then
trim. Fasten a woody stem, measuring the width of container just below
the rim, to the branch in Step 1. Step 1 is at a slightly backward slant,
Steps 2 and 3 face slightly forward. Cut the carnations in three different
lengths and arrange in a triangle.

PUSSY WILLOW—DAFFODILS

Materials Required

1. Slender vase 10″—14″ in height.
2. Two sprays of pussy willow.
   Substitutes : wisteria vine or slender flowering branches.
3. Three daffodils.
   Substitutes: narcissi, miniature lilies, tulips, roses, asters or anemones.
4. Short woody stem for support.
5. Florist wire.

Tall reaching lines of pussy willow create an upward rhythm in contrast to a low center of daffodils with their leaves furled. The arrangement is in an earthenware vase of subtle brown tones.

Method of Arrangement

Use only two sprays of willow to express the simplicity of this design. Curve as shown. Split the base of the taller willow and insert a woody stem measuring the width of the vase just below the rim. Place in the container facing slightly forward. Step 2 follows directly behind Step 1. Cut the daffodils in three different lengths and tie the blades to their stems with florist wire. Arrange in the vase with the blossoms facing one another in a triangle. Furl the blades slightly to soften their appearance. (See page 52)

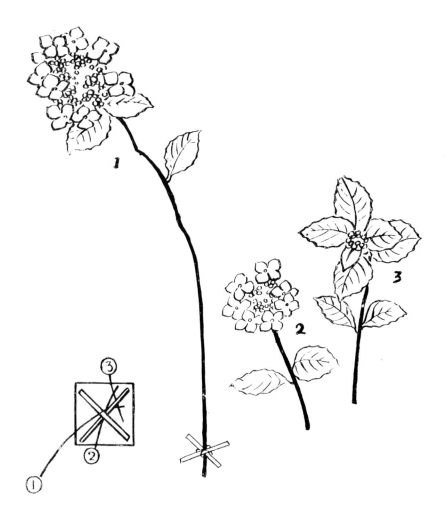

HYDRANGEAS

Materials Required

1. Vase 14"—16" in height.
   Bamboo, lacquer or wooden base.
2. Three hydrangea branches.
   Substitutes: giant chrysanthemums, sunflowers, peonies or large asters.
3. Two short woody stems for a cross support.
4. Florist wire.

Dainty clusters of pale blue hydrangea florets stand aloof from their thick leaves in a tall white vase, placed on a polished burl slab.

Method of Arrangement

Three hydrangea branches form a triangular design. Prune the dense leaves to avoid a cluttered appearance. Secure branch in Step 1 to a cross support with florist wire, then insert firmly in the vase, facing toward the left. Step 2 is placed off-center toward the left, and Step 3 at a backward slant to complete the triangular form. Use a short leafy branch for Step 3 to provide depth.

This is a good basic design for arranging large blossoms, or clusters of long-stemmed flowers.

DENDROBIUM ORCHIDS—FERNS

Materials Required

1. Vase 12″—16″ in height.
   Lacquer, bamboo or wooden base.
2. One or two sprays of orchids.
   Substitutes : roses or carnations.
3. Two asparagus ferns.
4. Woody stem for support.

Lacy ferns swirl around sprays of dendrobium orchids with airy
lightness. The black lacquer container and base accentuate the
simplicity of the arrangement.

Method of Arrangement

For the support use a tall sturdy branch and split the tip about two
inches. Support should be an inch below the rim of vase. Asparagus
ferns often require trimming to enhance their delicate lines. The tips of
the stems should taper off to give a more graceful appearance. When
trimming remove overlapping ferns by carefully pruning so as not to des-
troy the natural distribution of the foliage. Insert the stems in the split
support. Steps 1 and 2 are slightly forward. No more than five blossoms
should be used in a spray of orchids, or when using flowers individually.
Arrange in the center at a slightly backward slant.

How green the sunbeams
Reflected from the summer willow!
My cool white robes might be dyed in the tint,
If the rays should touch them.

                                        Kun-en

MORIBANA

Naturalistic Style

GLADIOLI

Materials Required

1. Rectangular, oval or square container 10″—12″.
   Lacquer or wooden base.
2. Two stems of gladioli with their leaves.
3. Pebbles.
4. Medium needle point holder.

Blossoms of yellow gladioli combined with their sword shaped leaves form a vertical design in an ancient bronze container placed on a lacquered scroll base. The Chinese porcelain figurine complements the simplicity of the composition.

Method of Arrangement

Rigid stems of the gladiolus can be cut down and their leaves regrouped. When shortening the stem, cut so as not to injure the leaves. The blossoms should be in different stages of development. Carefully remove most of the leaves and superfluous blossoms. The contour of each blossom should be clearly seen. The taller stem in Step 1 is inserted erect, and Step 2 at a slant, facing the center. The leaves are placed individually to envelop the flowers. Scatter pebbles at the base.

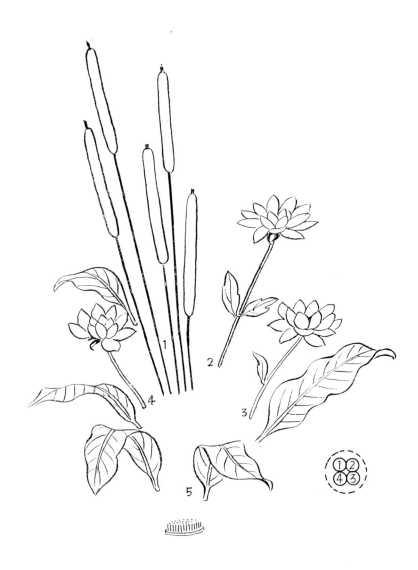

CATTAILS—DAHLIAS

Materials Required

1. Square, round or oval container 12″—14″.
2. Five cattails.
   Substitutes : sturdy reeds or rushes.
3. Three dahlias.
   Substitutes : chrysanthemums, large asters or peonies.
4. Five bird's-nest ferns.
   Substitutes : funkia, chard, philodendron, aspidistra or ti.
5. Pebbles.
6. Medium needle point holder.

Staggered heights of cattails and yellow dahlias radiate from a low center of bird's-nest ferns, in a pottery container of brown and green variegated tones. The composition is suggestive of crisp early autumn.

Method of Arrangement

Cut the cattails in various lengths and insert the tallest one at a backward slant, with the others following in line. All stems should emerge from a central point. Three dahlias form a triangle, with the stems almost free of leaves to accentuate their lines. Bird's-nest ferns are arranged low around the flowers and cattails. Each leaf is different in size. Scatter pebbles at the base.

DAFFODILS—RUSHES

Materials Required

1. Round or square container, preferably with lid.
   Rush mat, bamboo or wooden base.
2. Two daffodils with their leaves.
   Substitutes : narcissi or irises.
3. Five scouring rushes.
   Substitutes : sturdy reeds or rushes of similar form.
4. Pebbles.
5. Medium needle point holder.
6. Florist wire.

Trumpet daffodils combined with shoots of scouring rushes are arranged with extreme simplicity in an Oriental setting.

Method of Arrangement

Separate daffodils from their blades and rearrange as shown. If the sheaths are damaged, tie each group with florist wire. Wire should be completely concealed by pebbles. Step 1 is inserted upright, and Step 2 at a slant facing Step 1. Cut rushes in different lengths and place directly behind Step 1. Conceal the holder with pebbles. (See page 52)

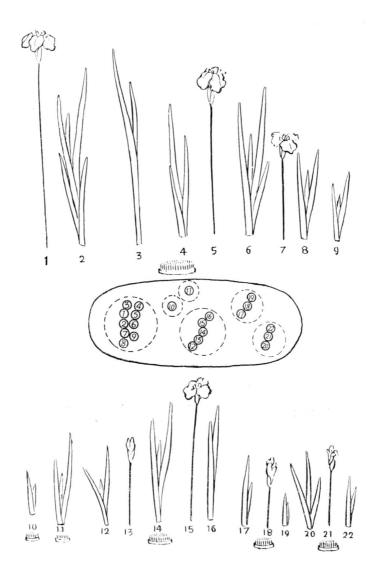

JAPANESE IRISES

Materials Required

1. Oval, rectangular or square container 16″—20″.
2. Seven irises with their leaves.
   Substitutes : daffodils or narcissi.
3. Three rocks different in shape and size ; and a scatter of pebbles.
4. One large, two medium, and three small needle point holders.

The atmosphere of a miniature pond is captured in this study of Japanese irises combined with rocks and pebbles in a white shallow bowl.

Method of Arrangement

The Heaven-Man-Earth principle is expressed in the placement of rocks. Heaven is characterized by a tall and large rock, Man by an intermediary rock, and Earth usually by a small flat rock. These are placed two together and a third apart. Never are they grouped symmetrically. Pebbles scattered at the base add to the realism of this miniature pond arrangement. This is known as a *fish-path* arrangement.

Select irises in different stages of development using four buds. Cut in varying lengths. The diagram gives a complete breakdown of the grouping of flowers and blades. (See page 53)

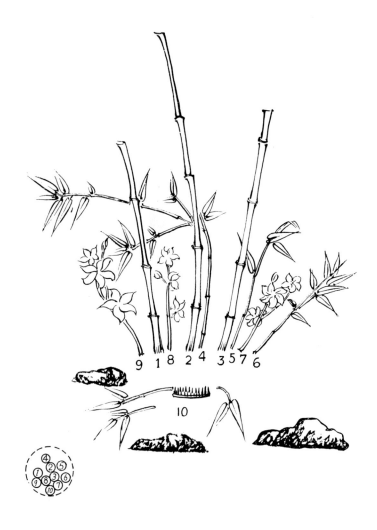

BAMBOO—FRANGIPANI

Materials Required

1. Oval or rectangular container 16″—20″.
2. Three bamboo stalks and three branches.
3. Clusters of frangipani.
    Substitutes : freesias, begonias, pompom chrysanthemums or clivia.
4. Three rocks different in size and shape, and a scatter of pebbles.
5. Large needle point holder.

Slender stalks of bamboo arranged with sparse leaves and clusters
of frangipani form an unusual design. The bamboo container
maintains the harmony of the bamboo motif in the arrangement.
Rocks and pebbles placed in the expanse of water create a feeling
of coolness.

Method of Arrangement

Select a tall slightly curved bamboo stalk and carefully remove the
leafy branches. Saw the stalk into three different lengths. These stalks
can be kept indefinitely although the color changes from green to yellowish
brown. Before inserting them in the holder, make several splits around
the base of each stalk to permit ease in handling. Place the stalks close
together with the tallest behind. The leafy branches are trimmed to create
an airy effect. The leaves are inserted behind the stalks to appear as part
of each parent stalk. Shorter leaves in Step 10 overhang behind the rocks.
Rocks surround the front part of the arrangement. A smaller rock is
placed to the left of the container, with a scatter of pebbles linking it with
the arrangement.

WEEPING WILLOW—NARCISSI

Materials Required

1. Rectangular or oval container 16″—20″.
2. Tall willow.
   Substitute: nandina with leafy branches.
3. Five narcissi with their leaves.
   Substitutes: daffodils, irises or tulips.
4. Cluster of boxwood.
   Substitutes: ferns, club moss, acacia or short shrubbery.
5. Pebbles.
6. One large and three small needle point holders.

Early spring is typified in this water reflecting arrangement of a tall willow spreading its graceful branches over slender narcissi. The deep blue porcelain container enhances the harmony of the composition.

Method of Arrangement

Willow limb should be studied to find its most appealing lines. All superfluous branches and conflicting lines should be removed. The final result must be delicate and graceful.

Split the base of the limb before inserting in the holder. Regroup the narcissi as shown. Flowers are different in height and should give the appearance that they are growing naturally (See page 52). Add a low cluster of boxwood, or substitute material, around the base of the willow. Scatter pebbles around Steps 4, 5 and 6 to conceal the holders.

This design is also pleasing without the willow, and can be used as a centerpiece on a low coffee table.

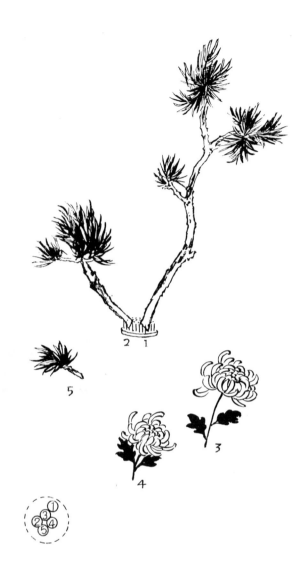

YEW—CHRYSANTHEMUMS

Materials Required

1. Round, oval or square container 12″—14″.
2. Three branches of yew.
   Substitute: pine or juniper.
3. Two chrysanthemums.
   Substitutes: dahlias, peonies, cannas or lilies.
4. Pebbles.
5. Medium needle point holder.

A study of bold angular lines of the yew which complement the exotic giant chrysanthemums is centered in a beige pottery bowl.

Method of Arrangement

The stark lines of yew branches give character to this arrangement. Trim to acquire the effect shown. Step 1 is at a backward slant and Step 2 forward. The chrysanthemums are cut short in different lengths and inserted in the center, Step 3 slightly backward, and Step 4 forward. Add a short branch to complete the triangular design. Conceal the holder with pebbles.

GERBERAS—BAMBOO—RIBBON GRASS

Materials Required

1. Oval or rectangular container 16″—20″.
2. Two slender dried bamboo roots.
   Substitutes: pussy willow, cattails, palm spires, bulrushes or scouring rushes.
3. Bunch of ribbon grass.
   Substitute: slender dracaena blades.
4. Five gerberas.
   Substitutes: daisies, zinnias, asters, pompom chrysanthemums or anemones.
5. Clusters of ferns.
   Substitutes: cedar, club moss or sprengeri.
6. Pebbles.
7. Two medium needle point holders.
8. Florist wire.

A double arrangement representing a woodland scene in a white porcelain bowl. This type of design is an incentive to new ideas for the artistic use of easily accessible floral combinations.

Method of Arrangement

Left group : Insert the bamboo roots as shown. When using substitute material which is not pliant, arrange upright and close together. Group a bunch of ribbon grass and tie it with florist wire. Each blade is different in height. Cover the holder with short ferns.

Right group : Cut five gerberas in different lengths and arrange as shown. Their foliage may be used instead of ferns. The two groups are linked with a scatter of pebbles.

MOCK ORANGE—ROSES

Materials Required

1. Round, square or oval basket with small receptacle for water, or a plain container.
2. Three branches of mock orange.
   Substitutes: flowering branch of similar form, or pussy willow.
3. Three roses.
   Substitutes: carnations, tulips or gerberas.
4. Pebbles.
5. Medium needle point holder.

Branches of mock orange peer over a low arrangement of roses in a bamboo basket. The Japanese feeling for extreme simplicity is well expressed in this composition.

Method of Arrangement

Cut three branches of mock orange in different lengths, trim and bend as shown. Insert them close together in the holder, following the same motion of line. The roses form a triangle, with Step 5 at a slightly backward slant. Add additional foliage at the base to give depth to the arrangement. Conceal the holder with pebbles.

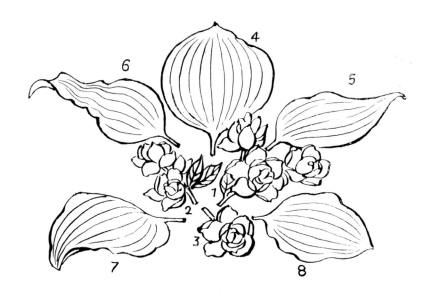

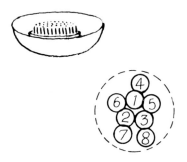

GARDENIAS—FUNKIA LEAVES

Materials Required

1. Small shallow bowl.
   Tapered wooden base or round mirror.
2. Cluster of gardenias.
   Substitutes: camellias, magnolias or cannas.
   Also, geraniums, freesias, frangipani, or tuberoses in a tight cluster.
3. Five funkia leaves.
   Substitutes: chard, aspidistra, canna or dracaena.
4. Large needle point holder.

A cluster of fragrant gardenias nestles in a circle of rich funkia foliage on a wormwood base in a centerpiece design.

Method of Arrangement

A shallow salad bowl is used for this arrangement and completely obscured by the funkia leaves. Cut the foliage short and arrange in an overlapping circle. The gardenias are inserted close together in the center. Part of their foliage is removed to avoid a cluttered appearance.

For a centerpiece on a low coffee table, use a round mirror to reflect the arrangement, or eliminate the base entirely.

Centerpieces are not typical Japanese designs. In a Japanese home arrangements are generally placed in the *tokonoma* (alcove) where they can be seen only from the front. In the western home, however, centerpieces are an important part of floral decoration, and for this reason the tri-linear pattern has been adapted to this type study.

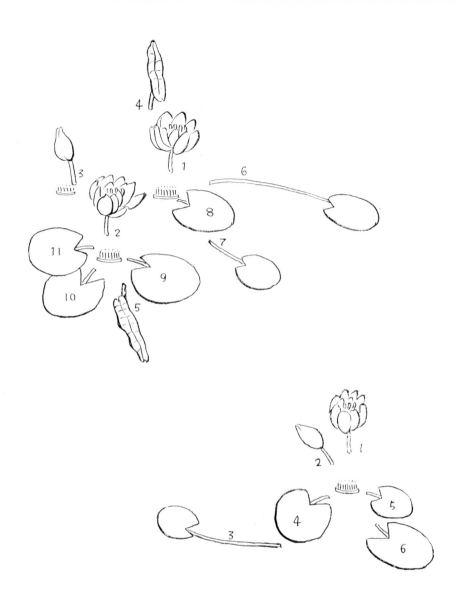

WATER LILIES

Materials Required

1. Rectangular, oval or square container 16″—20″.
    (For a smaller centerpiece use a small container and the left arrangement only.)
2. Three mature water lilies and two buds. Ten mature and two furled pads.
3. One small and three medium needle point holders.

Pink water lilies surrounded by their pads create an atmosphere of
pond life as they float in a deep blue porcelain container.
A symbolism often found in Japanese flower arrangements is illustrated
by the buds and immature furled pads, indicating a continuance of
plant life.

Method of Arrangement

This design is particularly suitable for a centerpiece on a hot summer
day.   Water lily pads and their blossoms must be cleansed thoroughly and
their stems pumped with cool water before arranging.   To add buoyancy
to the pads, massage them gently with your index finger and thumb, and
roll the edges slightly.   Arrange the pads around the blossoms overlapping
one another.   The long-stemmed pads and furled ones are placed under
the mature pads.

A drop of paraffin in the center of opened blossoms will prevent
them from closing in the evening.   Spray the arrangement to give a dewy
effect.

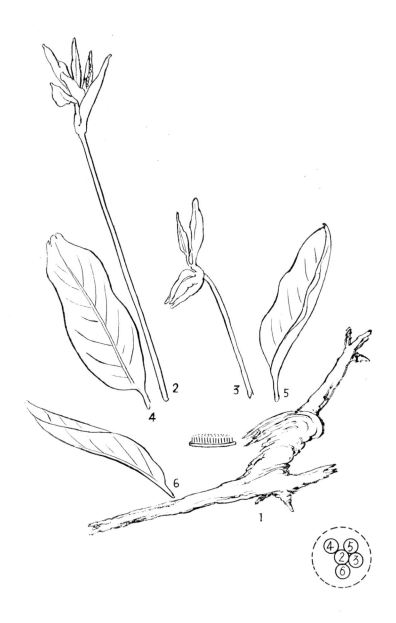

BIRDS OF PARADISE—DRIFTWOOD

Materials Required

1. Rectangular, square or round container 6″—8″.
   Rush mat, lacquer or wooden base.
2. Piece of driftwood horizontal in shape.
3. Two birds of paradise.
   Substitutes: amaryllis, gladioli, ginger or cannas.
4. Three leaves of birds of paradise.
   Substitutes: chard, palm, large maranta, dracaena or aspidistra.
5. Medium needle point holder.

Exotic birds of paradise rise in flight from a setting of their own rich foliage. The gnarled piece of driftwood on the rush mat adds to the feeling of flight. A study of dramatic simplicity.

Method of Arrangement

Balance a piece of similar driftwood on the rim of container. Drift-wood should partially conceal the container. Cut the birds of paradise in contrasting heights. Step 2 is at a backward slant, and Step 3 forward. The leaves are also different in size and height and are arranged to envelop the flowers.

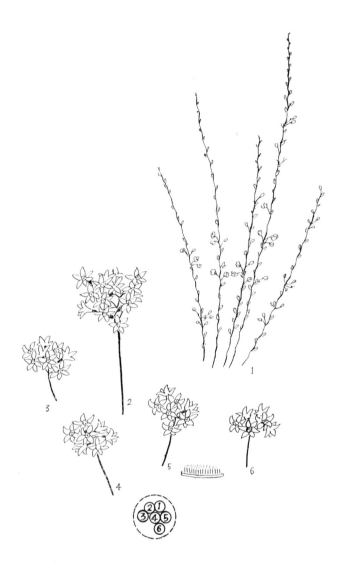

FLOWERING PLUM—NARCISSI

Materials Required

1. Round or square container 6"—8", preferably with lid.
   Rush mat, bamboo or wooden base.
2. Five branches of plum.
   Substitutes: flowering branch of similar form, scotch broom or willow.
3. Clusters of narcissi.
   Substitutes: clivia, hydrangeas, frangipani or geraniums.
4. Pebbles.
5. Medium needle point holder.

Flowering plum branches rise in irregular lengths from a low arrangement of narcissi. The lacquer candy bowl, with its lid tilted against
the container on the bamboo mat, lends a note of charm to the
composition.

Method of Arrangement

Cut the plum branches in varying lengths and bend each branch as
shown. The lines should emerge from a central point, rising upward. Each
cluster of blossoms is different in height and placed close together. Conceal
the holder with pebbles.

LOQUAT—CALLA LILIES

Materials Required

1. Oval or rectangular container 16″—20″.
2. Three loquat branches.
   Substitutes: rhododendron, magnolia, or pittisporum.
3. Five miniature callas with their foliage.
   Substitutes: tulips, pompom chrysanthemums, zinnias, asters, gerberas or begonias.
4. Pebbles.
5. Medium needle point holder.

Leafy tipped branches of loquats diverge from a low composition of
miniature calla lilies with their foliage in a white porcelain bowl.

Method of Arrangement

This is a typical Japanese basic design adaptable to a variety of
floral materials.

Three loquat branches form a triangle. Branches are impaled at a
slant rather than upright. At the tips of the branches some leaves are
removed or trimmed to avoid a top-heavy appearance. Below the tips, the
branches are stripped completely. Cut the lilies short in varying lengths,
and with Steps 4, 5 and 8 form another triangle within the branches. The
calla leaves are placed low around the lilies. Scatter pebbles at the base.

ANTHURIUMS—SOLOMON'S SEAL

Materials Required

1. Small shell or container 6"—8", round or oval.
   Use a small round or oval base to give contrast to shell.
2. Two anthuriums with small spathes.
   Substitute: spray of orchids.
3. Two leafy stems of Solomon's seal.
   Substitutes: miniature philodendrons, bridal wreath or ferns.
4. Small needle point holder.

A feeling of arrested motion is expressed in the brilliant coral
anthuriums which emerge from a leafy base of Solomon's seal.
The coral tones of the sea shell, set on a black lacquer base, reflect
a subtle harmony of composition.

Method of Arrangement

Cut the anthuriums in contrasting heights, and curve the taller one
as shown. The flowers are inserted in the center with Step 1 at a backward
slant and Step 2 forward. The spathes face each other. Arrange leafy
stems to surround the flowers in a semi-circle.

When arranging a spray of orchids insert stem in the center following
the line of the taller anthurium.

WISTERIA TENDRILS—TUBEROSES

Materials Required

1. Small receptacle to hold water. (A coffee can painted brown, black or green makes an ideal container.)
   Dried palm sheath or large banana leaf.
2. Two wisteria tendrils.
   Substitutes: willow, scotch broom or bitter-sweet.
3. Clusters of tuberoses.
   Substitutes: freesias, jasmine or begonias.
4. Ferns.
5. Medium needle point holder.

Wisteria tendrils float gracefully in rising motion behind clusters of fragrant tuberoses arranged in a palm sheath.

Method of Arrangement

The natural lines of wisteria have a treasure of possibilities. Select two curved ones and arrange them in a similar rhythmic manner to give the design height and grace. Cut the flowers in varying lengths, not taller than the predominating lines of the wisteria, and arrange as shown. Tie a few narrow blades with florist wire, and place directly behind the tallest group of flowers. Cut the ferns short and insert around the blossoms.

A centerpiece can be created with this design by eliminating the wisteria tendrils. Arrange the blossoms as shown, but insert the tallest group at a backward slant to achieve a semi-circle effect.

MAGNOLIAS—DRIED LIMB

Materials Required

1. Small receptacle to hold water.
   Rectangular lacquer or wooden base.
2. Three magnolia branches with three blossoms.
3. Vertical dried limb or driftwood.
4. Pebbles.
5. Large needle point holder.

Magnolia blossoms, when combined with a tall branch, give a feeling of natural harmony. The lacquer base complements the glistening foliage in subtle contrast.

Method of Arrangement

Nail a tall vertical limb to a flat board as shown. Place directly behind a small container.

The branches are cut fairly short in three varying lengths. The tallest in Step 2 is inclined at a backward slant, Step 3 in the center, and Step 4 toward the left. Prune branches carefully to remove some of the basal leaves so that the flowers will stand apart from their foliage. The container should be completely concealed by the foliage. (Without the tall limb, this design makes an effective centerpiece. Add additional blossoms for depth.)

AZALEAS—CHRYSANTHEMUMS

Materials Required

1. Triangular, square or round container 10″—12″.
2. Three azalea branches.
   Substitutes: flowering branch of similar form.
3. Two chrysanthemums.
   Substitutes: lilies, tulips or irises.
4. Medium needle point holder.

Bright azaleas ascend in a sweeping curve around two white chrysanthemums, placed in a triangular bamboo container.

Method of Arrangement

To acquire a crescent design with azaleas, the natural curves of the branches should be emphasized by removing conflicting lines. From a comparatively heavy concentration at the base the azalea branches thin out as they rise. For contrast, two chrysanthemums are added in the center. These are in uneven heights. Step 4 is inclined at a backward slant and Step 5 in the center. When using a round or square container, a third flower should be added between Steps 4 and 5, and placed at a backward slant.

ASPIDISTRA—TIGER LILIES

Materials Required

1. Round or square container 12″—14″.
2. Seven aspidistra leaves.
   Substitutes: dracaena, ti or bird's-nest ferns.
3. Tiger lily and bud.
   Substitutes: cannas, amaryllis or calla lilies.
4. Clusters of bouvardia.
   Substitutes: acacia, candy tuft, club moss or ferns.
5. Pebbles.
6. Large needle point holder.

Furled leaves of aspidistra with clusters of bouvardia encircle a tiger lily and bud in a flaming red and black lacquer bowl.

Method of Arrangement

Three tall aspidistra leaves are furled and tied at the base with florist wire to hold them together. The shorter leaves are arranged overlapping one another to complete the crescent design, leaving sufficient space in the center for the lily and bud, (see page 51). To give leaves a glossy appearance, oil them with a rag. Insert the flowers erect, and clusters of bouvardia low, to the right. Scatter pebbles at the base.

NEW ZEALAND FLAX—DAHLIAS

Materials Required

1. Oval or round container 12"—14".
2. Five tall blades of New Zealand flax.
   Substitutes: yucca, pandanus, sansevieria or iris blades.
3. Two dahlias.
   Substitutes: peonies, amaryllis, cannas, chrysanthemums or lilies.
4. Short sprigs of pine.
   Substitutes: leather ferns or podocarpus.
5. Pebbles.
6. Medium needle point holder.
7. Florist wire.

Staggered heights of New Zealand flax soar upward in contrast to two
variegated red dahlias, with pine massed at the base. The oval shape
of the lacquer bowl creates a well balanced contour of design.

Method of Arrangement

Grade five blades as shown. Assemble with the base of each blade
overlapping the other, and tie with florist wire. The dahlias are cut in
different lengths. Step 2 is placed upright and Step 3 slightly forward.
Add sprigs of pine to the right of the arrangement. Scatter pebbles at
the base.

NOMENCLATURE OF PLANTS

POPULAR JAPANESE & ENGLISH TERMS

Ajisai..................... Hydrangea

Akabansis .... Agapanthus
Lily-of-the-Nile
African Lily

Amariris .... Amaryllis
Belladonna Lily

Anturiamu.................. Anthurium
Flamingo

Asagao .... Morning Glory
Blue Dawnflower

Asparagus .... Ferns (Asparagus Plumosus)

Bara .... Rose

Boke .... Flowering Quince

Buvardia .... Bouvardia
'President Garfield'

Daria .... Dahlia

Enishida .... Scotch Broom

Fuji .... Wisteria

Fujizuru................... Wisteria Vine

Futoi .... Bulrush
Club-rush

Gabera .... Gerbera
Barberton Daisy
Transvaal Daisy

Gakumoso .... Ribbon Grass
(Chlorophytum Capense)

Gama .... Cattails
Reed Mace

Gradioras (To-shobu) .... Gladiolus

Giboshi .... Funkia Leaves
Hosta Leaves

Gokurakucho .... Bird of Paradise
Strelitzia

(132)

Hakuren	Magnolia
Hagi......................	Bush Clover
Haran	Aspidistra Evergreen Room Plant
Hasu	Lotus
Ibuki	Juniper
Iris	Iris (Dutch)
Jinchoge	Daphne
Shikuramen................	Cyclamen
Kakitsubata	Iris (Laevigata)
Kaneshon	Carnation
Kayu (Kara)	Calla Lily
Keshi	Oriental Poppy
Kiku	Chrysanthemum
Kiri	Paulownia
Kingyoso	Snapdragon
Kirinso	Golden Rod
Kodemari.................	Maiden's Wreath Bridal Wreath Francoa Spirea Spiraea
Konyaku	Grape Hyacinth Muscari
Kuchi-nashi	Gardenia
Kunshiran	Clivia Caffre Lily
Maki	Yew
Matsu	Pine
Miriogratus	Ferns (Asparagus Myriocladus)
Miyakowasure.............	Aster
Momiji	Japanese Maple

Momo	Flowering Peach
Nadeshiko	Pink Dianthus
Narukoran	Solomon's Seal
Nanten	Nandin Heavenly Bamboo
Nashi	Flowering Pear
Neko Yanagi	Pussy Willow
Nuzairan	New Zealand Flax
Ominaeshi	Patrina
Omoto	Japanese Rhodea
Ran	Orchid
Rappa Suisen	Trumpet Daffodil
Rikyubai	Mock Orange
Sakura	Cherry Blossoms
Sanseberia	Sansevieria Snake Plant
Shakunage	Rhododendron
Shakuyaku	Peony
Shobu	Iris (Kaempferi)
Sotetsu	Cycas Palm Sago Palm
Sugi	Japanese Cedar
Suisen	Narcissus
Suiren	Water Lily
Susuki	Pampas Flowering Grass
Take	Bamboo
Take no ne	Bamboo Roots
Taniwatari	Bird's Nest-Fern
Tenmondo	Ferns (Lucidus Asparagus)

Tokusa	Scouring Rush Horsetail
Tsubaki	Camellia
Toritome	Tritoma Kniphofia
Tsuge.....................	Japanese Box
Tsutsuji	Azalea
Tuberose	Tuberose
Turipu	Tulip
Ume	Plum Blossoms
Yama Zakura	Wild Cherry Blossoms
Yanagi	Willow
Yuki Yanagi	Spirea
Yuri	Lily